Pebble® Plus

Countries

India

by Christine Juarez

Consulting Editor: Gail Saunders-Smith, PhD

CAPSTONE PRESS
a capstone imprint

Pebble Plus is published by Capstone Press,
1710 Roe Crest Drive, North Mankato, Minnesota 56003
www.capstonepub.com

Library of Congress Cataloging-in-Publication Data
Juarez, Christine, 1976–
  India / by Christine Juarez.
      pages cm.—(Pebble plus. Countries)
  Summary: "Simple text and full-color photographs illustrate the land, animals, and people of India"—Provided by publisher.
  Includes bibliographical references and index.
  ISBN 978-1-4765-4227-0 (library binding)—ISBN 978-1-4765-6042-7 (ebook PDF)
1. India—Juvenile literature. I. Title.
DS407.J83 2014
954—dc23
                                                    2013031476

Editorial Credits
Erika L. Shores, editor; Bobbie Nuytten, designer; Tracy Cummins, media researcher; Laura Manthe, production specialist

Photo Credits
Getty Images: The India Today Group, 5; iStockphotos: paresh3d, 22; Shutterstock: 29151112, 4, Aleksandar Todorovic, 1, Dmitry Kalinovsky, 11, Eduard Kyslynskyy, 9, GreenTree, 22, Im Perfect Lazybones, 17, JeremyRichards, 15, Joe Gough, 13, Jorg Hackemann, 19, Mazzzur, 21, Ohmega1982, back cover (globe), OPIS Zagreb, 7, Transia Design, cover, 1 (design element), turtix, cover,

Note to Parents and Teachers

The Countries set supports national social studies standards related to people, places, and culture. This book describes and illustrates India. The images support early readers in understanding the text. The repetition of words and phrases helps early readers learn new words. This book also introduces early readers to subject-specific vocabulary words, which are defined in the Glossary section. Early readers may need assistance to read some words and to use the Table of Contents, Glossary, Read More, Internet Sites, and Index sections of the book.

Printed in the United States of America in North Mankato, Minnesota.
092013   007775CGS14

Table of Contents

Where Is India?

India is a country in southern Asia. It is almost twice the size of the U.S. state of Alaska. New Delhi is India's capital city.

Landforms

India has many landforms. To the
north are the Ganges River and
the Himalayas. The Thar Desert
is to the west. Mountains line the
southwest and southeast coasts.

Animals

India has all kinds of animals.

Tigers and elephants roam India.

Cobras and other snakes live there.

Colorful birds like peacocks and

parrots make homes there too.

Language and Population

India is home to more than

1.2 billion people. Most people

live in small houses in rural villages.

People speak Hindi, English,

or one of 14 other languages.

Food

Indians put a spicy, creamy sauce called curry on vegetables and meats. People sometimes scoop food with a flat bread called chapatti. Rice is often eaten with meals.

Celebrations

National holidays are important in India. Republic Day is January 26. Independence Day is August 15. People watch parades on these days.

Where People Work

Most Indians work as farmers. They grow rice and wheat. In cities, Indians work in factories that make clothing. People work in business or with computers.

Transportation

Indians ride motorcycles
or bicycles. They also travel
by cycle rickshaw. A driver pedals
a bicycle while pulling a cart
with one or two riders.

Famous Sight

About 400 years ago,
20,000 workers and hundreds
of elephants built the Taj Mahal.
It took 22 years to finish. It is
India's most famous building.

Country Facts

Name: Republic of India

Capital: New Dehli

Population: 1,220,800,359 (July 2013 estimate)

Size: 1,147,950 square miles (2,973,177 square kilometers)

Languages: Hindi, English, and 14 other official languages

Main Crops: rice, wheat, cotton, tea

India's flag

Money: rupee

Critical Thinking Using the Common Core

1. Look at page 4. What does the author tell you about the city starred on the map? (Craft and Structure)

2. What are some of the foods that are shown on page 13? How do they compare to the foods you eat on a daily basis? (Integration of Knowledge and Ideas)

Glossary

capital—the city in a country where the government is based

coast—land next to an ocean or sea

cobra—a venomous snake

desert—a dry area with very little rain

factory—the place where a product is made

Himalyas—a mountain range in Asia; the world's tallest mountain, Mount Everest, is found in the Himalyas

landform—a natural feature of the land

language—the way people speak or talk

rural—having to do with the countryside

Read More

Bajaj, Varsha. *T Is for Taj Mahal: An India Alphabet*. Ann Arbor, Mich.: Sleeping Bear Press, 2011.

Kalman, Bobbie. *India. The People*. The Lands, Peoples, and Cultures Series. New York: Crabtree Pub., 2010.

Internet Sites

FactHound offers a safe, fun way to find Internet sites related to this book. All of the sites on FactHound have been researched by our staff.

Here's all you do:
Visit *www.facthound.com*
Type in this code: 9781476542270

Check out projects, games and lots more at **www.capstonekids.com**

Index

Word Count: 235   Grade: 1   Early-Intervention Level: 20